MANGA UNIVERSITY

"A Day in the Life of a Japanese Schoolgirl"

Manga University Presents...

Costume Collection: A Day in the Life of a Japanese Schoolgirl

Copyright © 2003 Ginga Shuppan Co., Ltd.

This English edition is an anthology of the "Costume Pose Collection" series first published in 1999-2000 by Ginga Shuppan Co., Ltd.
English edition published in 2003 by Ginga Shuppan Co., Ltd.
1F Nikken Buiding, 75 Waseda-cho,
Shinjuku-ku, Tokyo 162-0042, Japan
http://www.ginga-jp.com

Executive Producer: Nobuyuki Takahashi (Studio Hard)
Production Manager: Haruhiko Kaneko
Japanese Series Editor: Kiyoshi Takenaka
Photographers: Hisasi Maruyama, Masaki Kon
English Edition Editor: Glenn Kardy (Japanime Co., Ltd.)
English Edition Layout Editor: Satoshi Ide (Ginga Shuppan Co., Ltd.)
English Edition Translation: Kanako Umehara (Japanime Co., Ltd.)

Distributed by
Japanime Co., Ltd.
2-8-12 Naka-cho, Kawaguchi-shi,
Saitama 332-0022, Japan
Phone/Fax: +81-(0)48-259-3444
E-mail: sales@japanime.com
http://www.mangauniversity.com

First printing: June 2003

ISBN4-87777-051-8
Printed and Bound in Japan by Toppan Printing Co., Ltd.

FOREWORD

Pose-reference books for manga artists have been around since the 1980s. However, the "Costume Pose Collection" series published by Ginga Shuppan differs from other such books in that it shows each pose from several angles rather than just one. Specifically, the models were photographed from eight different directions and three different angles, for a total of 24 photographs per pose. By providing these multiple views, we hope to make it easier for artists to draw realistic manga characters.

"A Day in the Life of a Japanese Schoolgirl" is an English-language anthology of five of the "Costume Pose Collection" books: "School Uniforms," "School Sportswear," "Waitresses and Maids," "Kimono" and "Pajamas." Although we had to exclude some photographs found in those books when assembling this anthology, our concept remains the same, with each pose depicted from eight different directions.

We encourage artists to use this book as a reference when sketching and composing characters. The photographs can also be traced. If you find this book helpful in the creation of your manga, you are certainly free to mention the book on your credits page (though doing so is not mandatory). We also welcome your feedback and requests, which you may submit to our editorial department.

Haruhiko Kaneko
President
Ginga Shuppan
Tokyo

SECTION 1
GOOD MORNING

Hikari Okamoto

Born: Aug. 9, 1982
Blood Type: AB
In addition to her work as a model, Hikari is an accomplished vocalist and has performed at various Tokyo-area nightclubs. Her singing ability coupled with her innocent and unique personality has won her a solid fan base.

W aking up is hard to do—especially for a Japanese schoolgirl. Each and every weekday, a seemingly endless marathon of pop quizzes and extracurricular activities awaits her. She leaves for school at 7 a.m. and doesn't return home until dinner is served, after which she'll spend several more hours doing homework and preparing for grueling college entrance exams. (She'll be lucky to be asleep by 2 a.m.) And on this particular day, she's interviewing for a part-time job as well. Let's just hope she didn't get up on the wrong side of the futon!

In this section, we'll watch Hikari Okamoto as she goes through her early morning routine. After tossing and turning for a few minutes, Hikari manages to pull herself out of bed and begin her stretching exercises. A cup of strong coffee (no cream or sugar—gotta count those calories!) gives her the jolt she'll need to make it through the first part of the day. Then it's time to brush her teeth, get dressed and get going.

Toss and Turn 1-2

Rise and Shine! 1-2

006-009

010-013

Moning Coffee

Time to Brush

014-015

016-017

■Toss and Turn ①

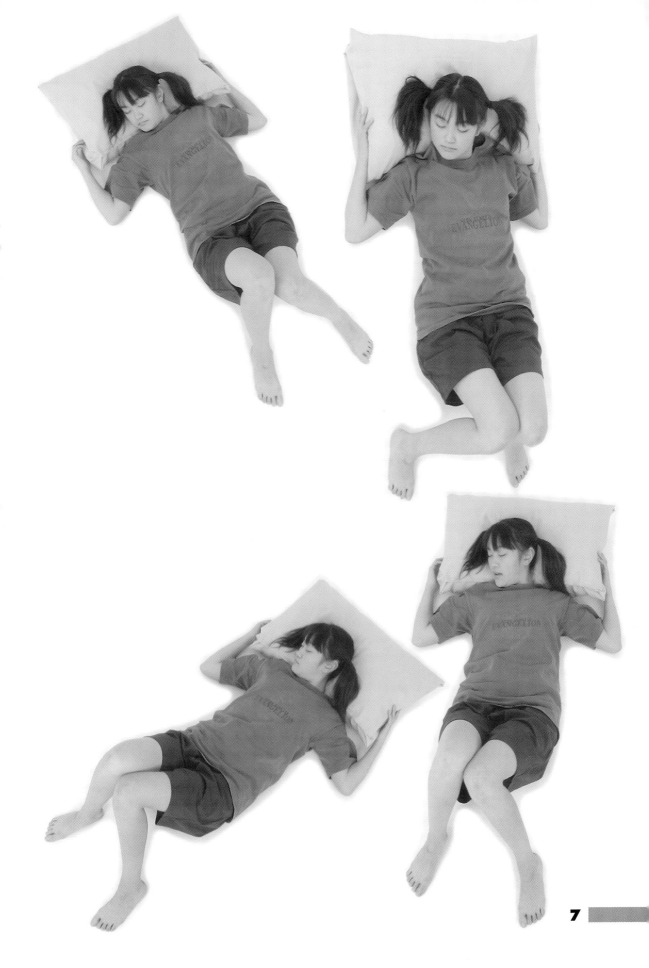

Rise and Shine! ②

■Morning Coffee

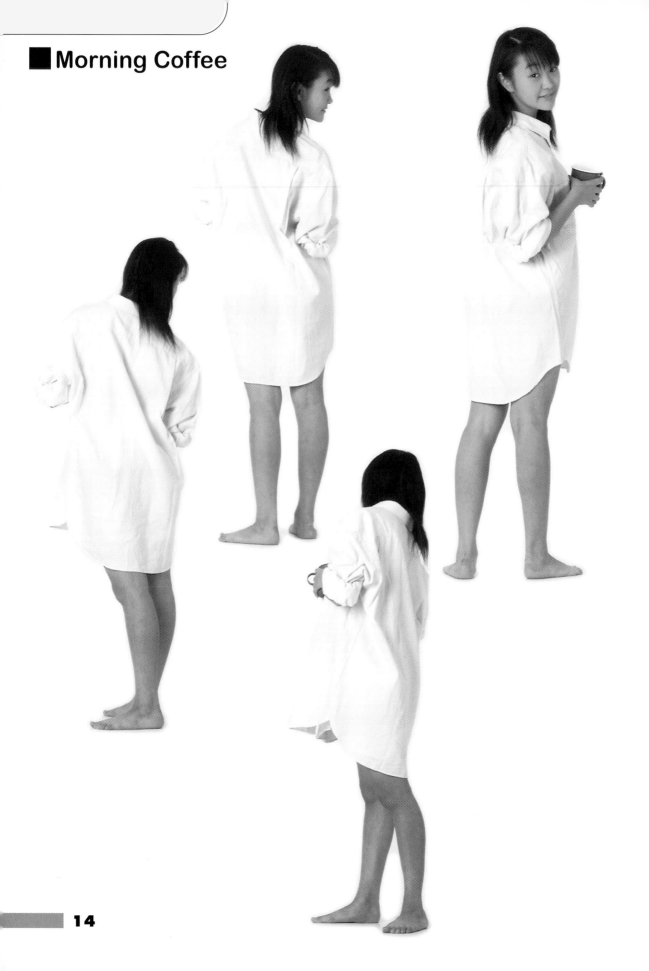

■Time to Brush

GOOD MORNING

Close-ups

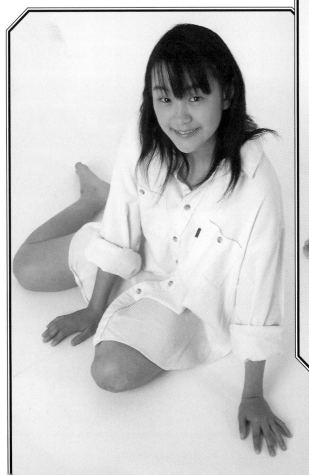

SECTION 2
SCHOOL DAYS

Mami Aida

Born: Oct. 31, 1983
Blood Type: A
A multitalented performer, Mami has appeared in musicals, television commercials, magazine advertisements and fashion shows. She made her debut at a young age in a commercial for McDonald's, and is considered by many to be a rising star in the Japanese entertainment industry.

Chinatsu Mori

Born: Nov. 7, 1978
Blood Type: O
Chinatsu is a favorite on the "campaign girl" circuit, having been featured on the covers of national magazines. She is honing her talents as a voice actress, and intends to explore a career as a television actress as well.

Riasu Arama

Born: Jan. 23, 1983
Blood Type: O
Gifted with a unique, friendly voice, Riasu enjoys popularity as the star of her own radio program. She also has appeared on television variety shows, and has lent her vocal talents to several videogame soundtracks. She occasionally poses for Japanese magazines.

Most Japanese schoolgirls spend about seven hours a day in their regular classrooms. Of course, that doesn't include the hour or two devoted to after-school music lessons or volleyball practice, two hours each evening in *juku* (cram schools), and the midnight study sessions at home. Is it any wonder that so many of Japan's *onna-no-ko* are living in a daze?

Over the next several pages we'll get up-close and personal with Mami Aida, whose straight-A attitude and impeccable sense of schoolgirl style has earned her the title "Teacher's Pet." Next, we'll get physical in the gymnasium with Chinatsu Mori (pages 042-045), fool around with class clown Riasu Arama (pages 046-049), and finally spend some quality time with Riasu in after-school detention (pages 050-055).

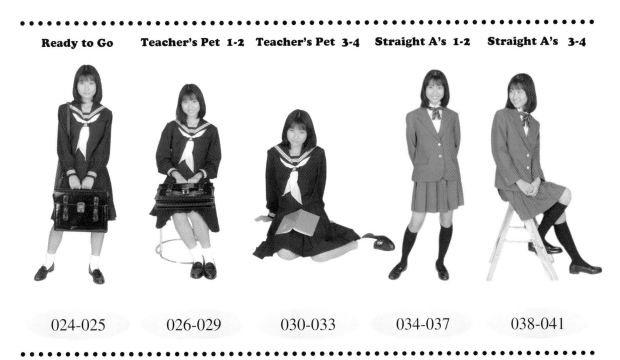

Ready to Go **Teacher's Pet 1-2** **Teacher's Pet 3-4** **Straight A's 1-2** **Straight A's 3-4**

024-025   026-029   030-033   034-037   038-041

In the Gym   **Go Team!**   **Class Clown 1-2**   **After-School Detention 1-3**

042-043   044-045   046-049   050-055

■Ready to Go

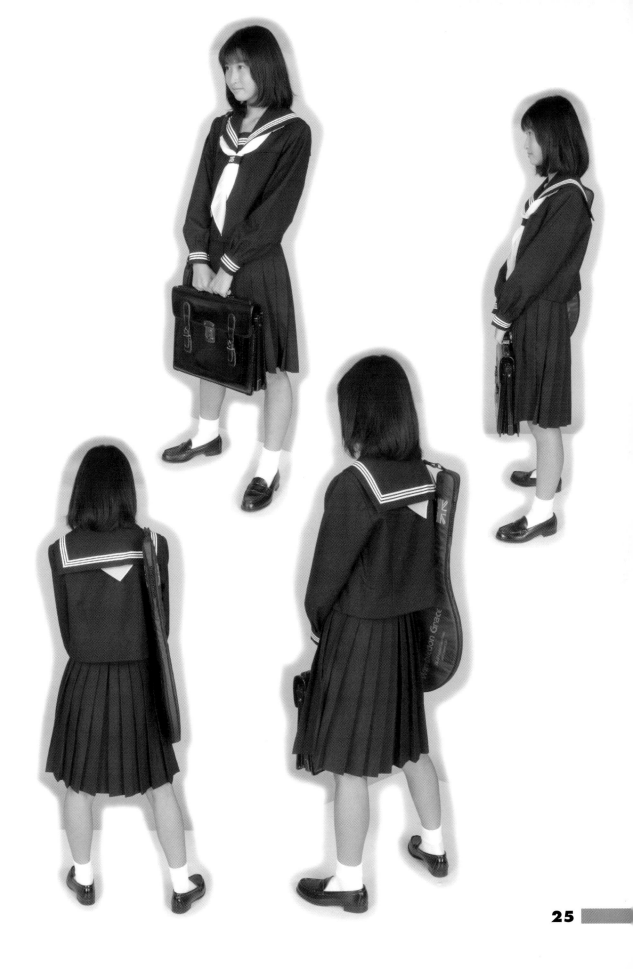

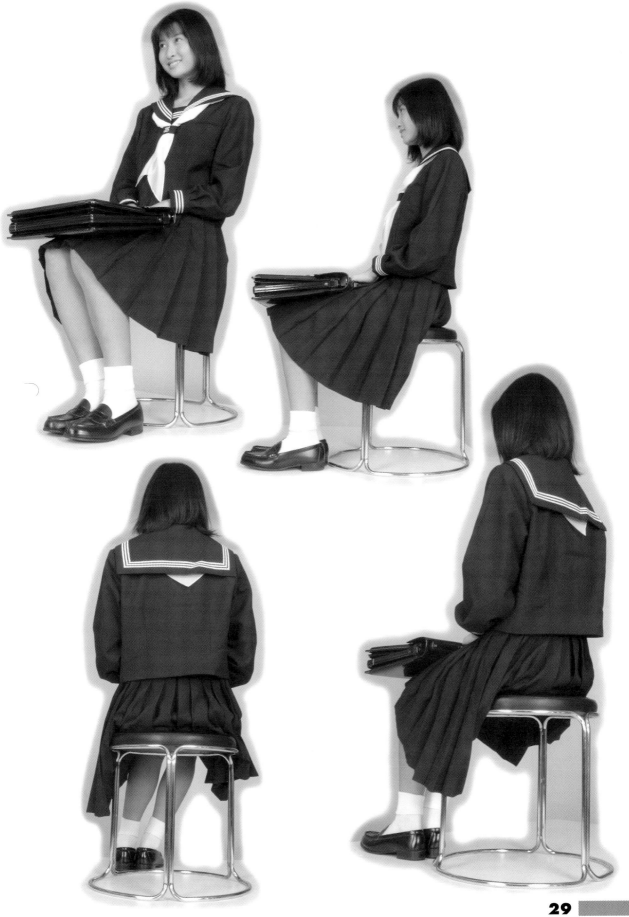

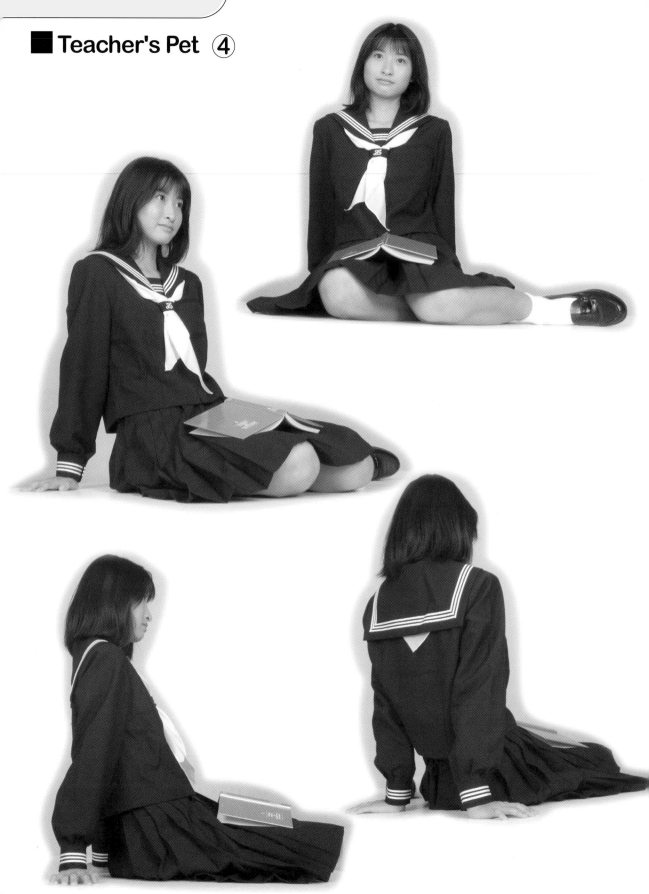

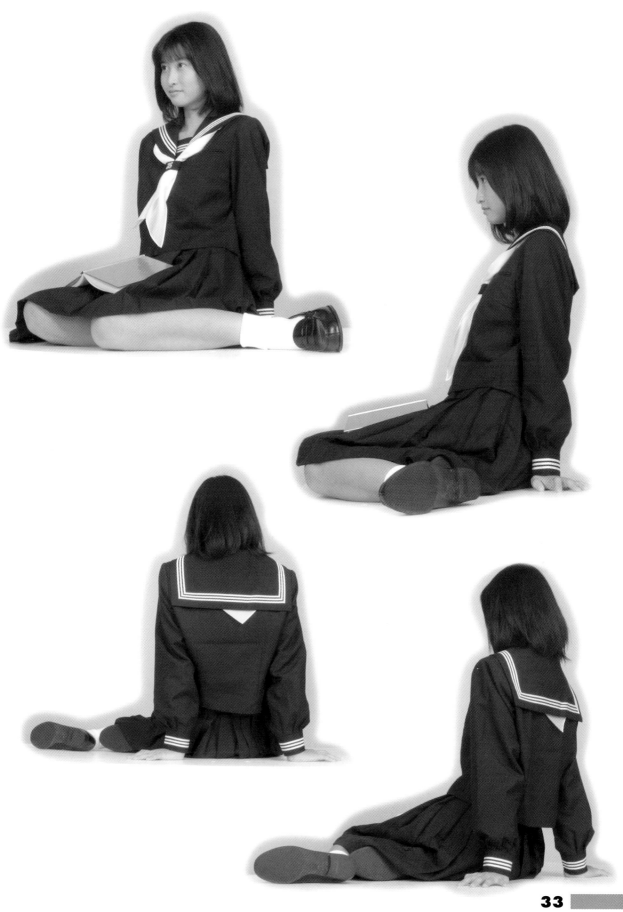

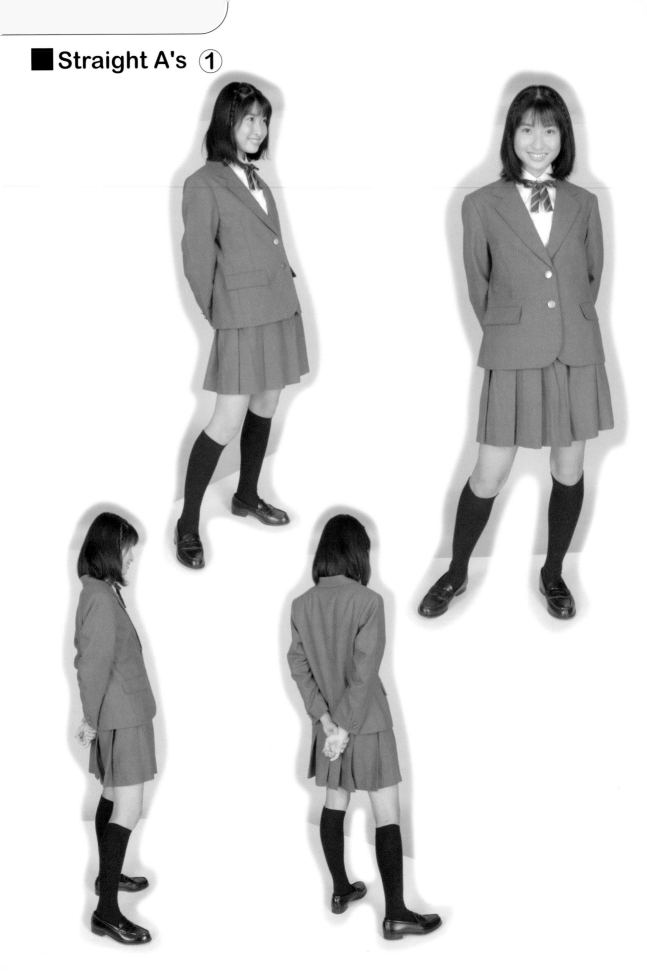

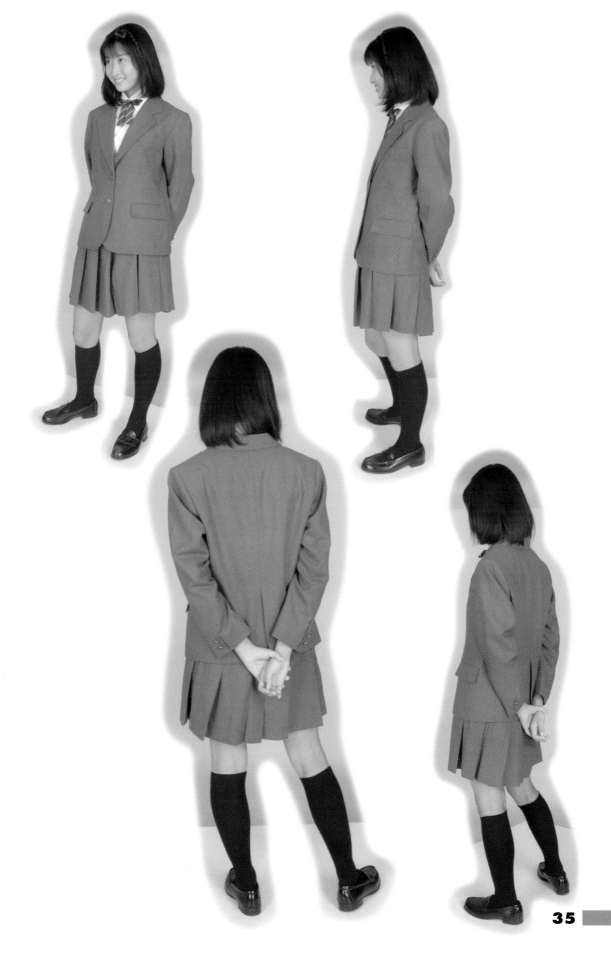

■Straight A's ②

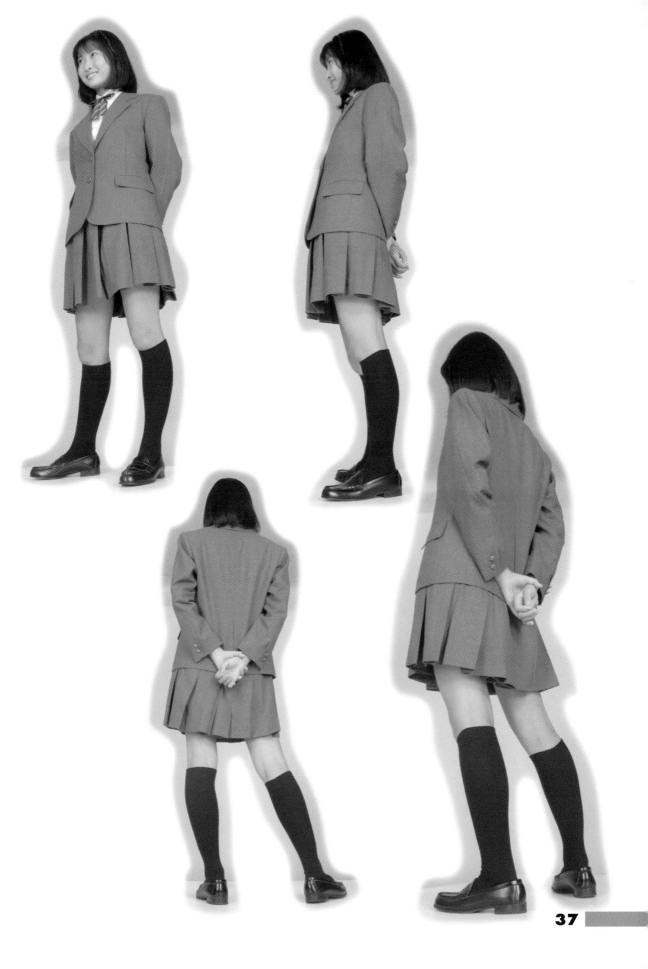

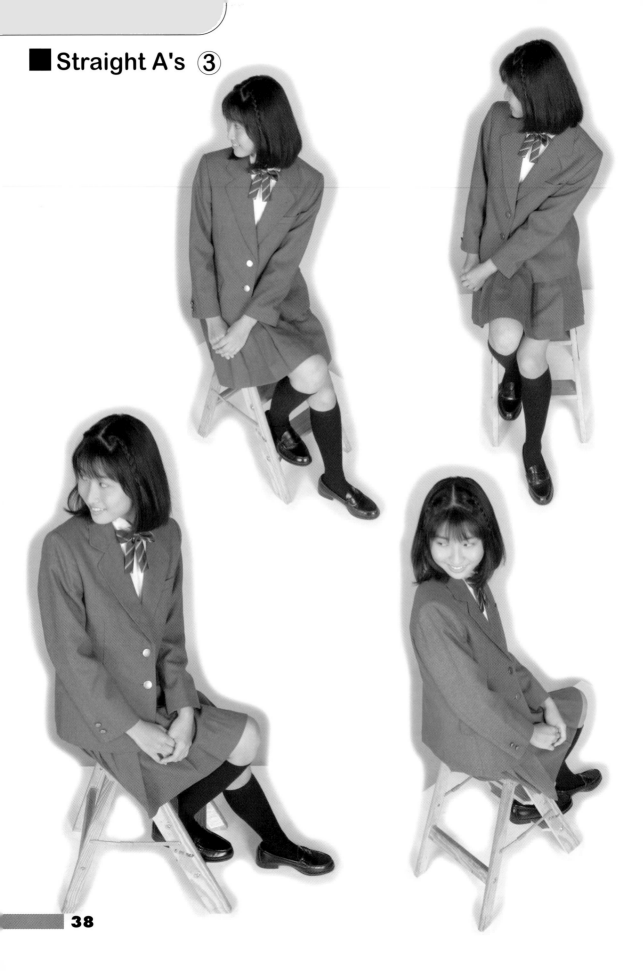

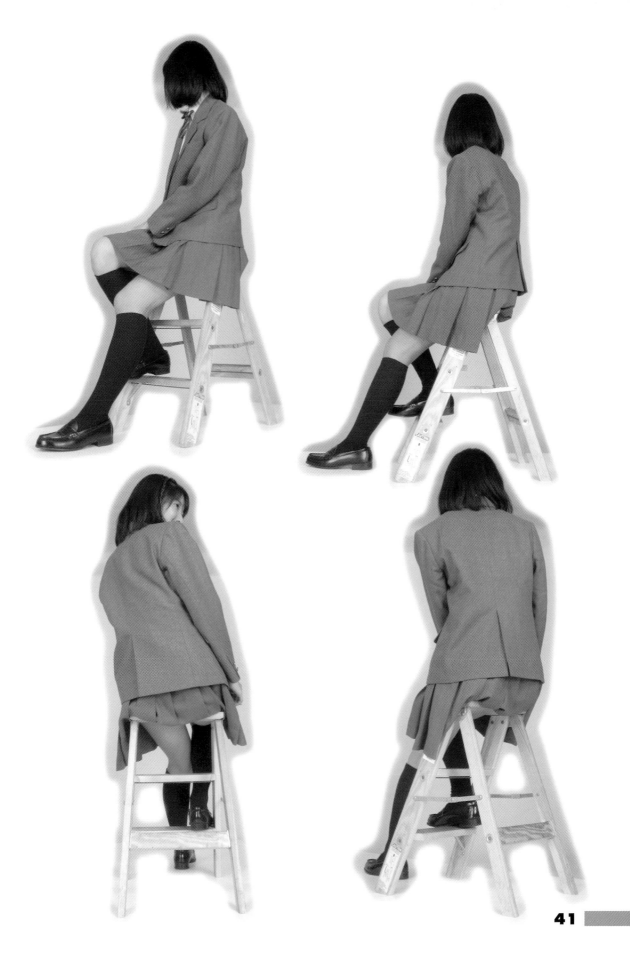

■Go Team!

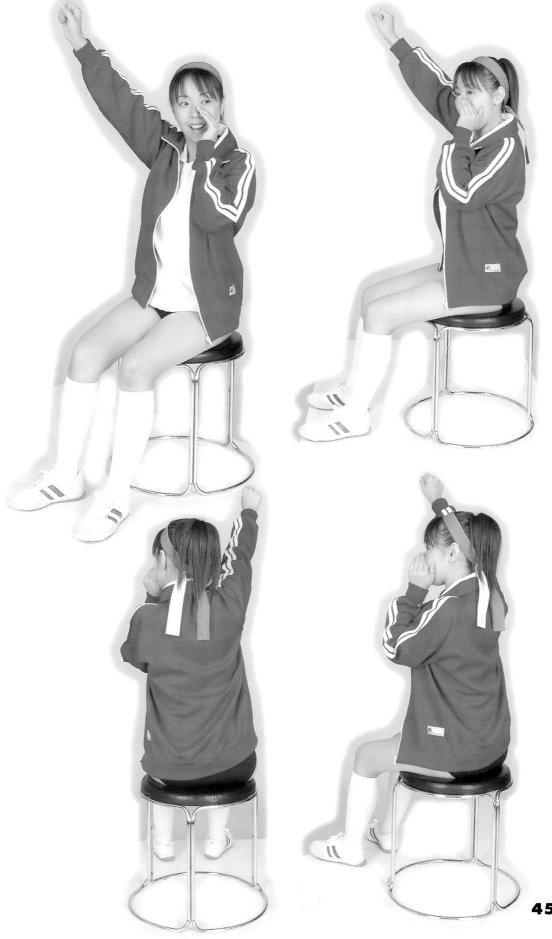

■Class Clown ①

■Class Clown ②

■After-School
Detention ①

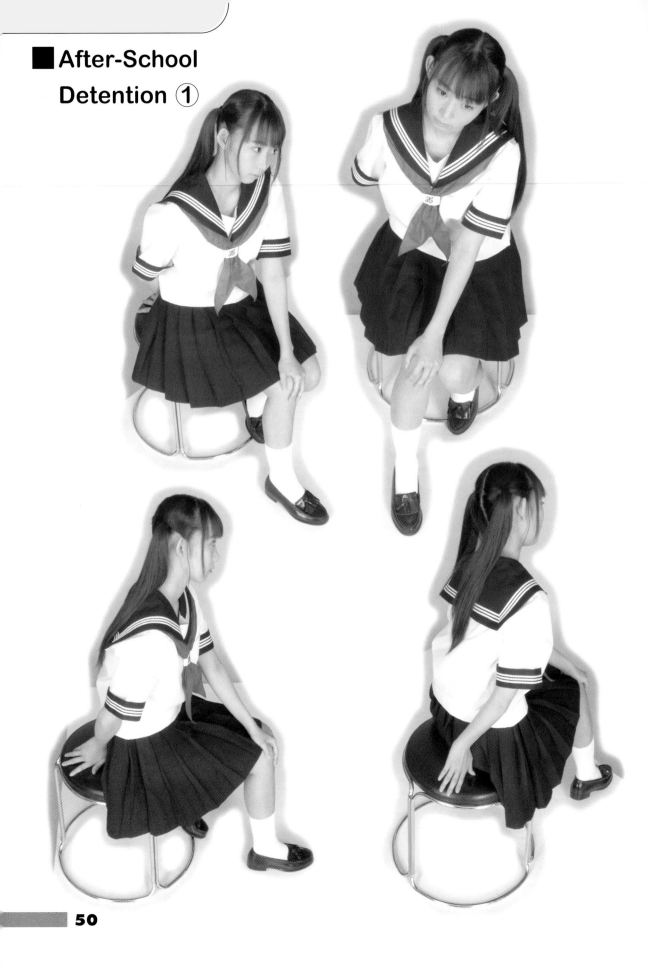

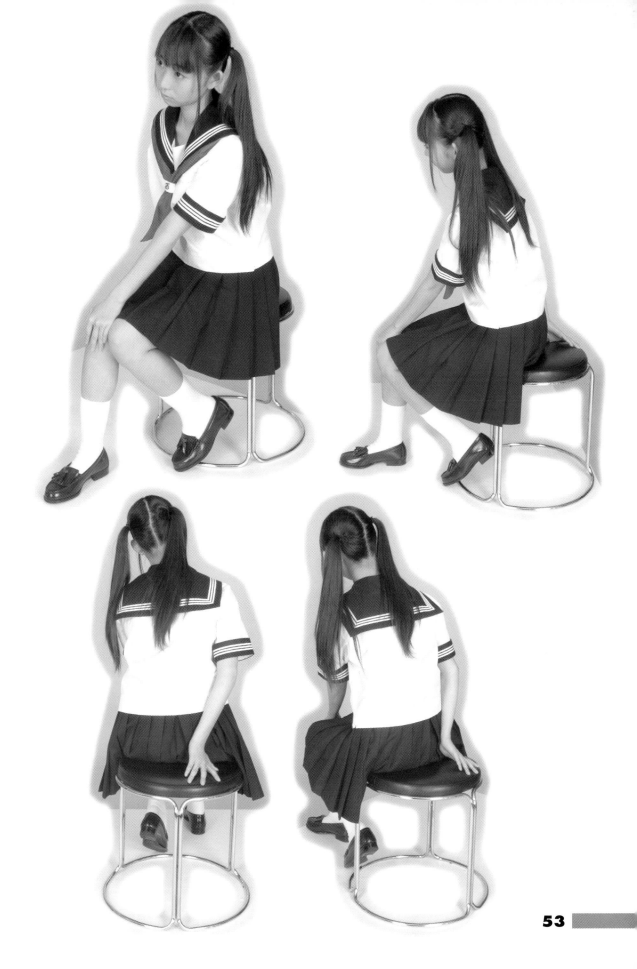

■After-School Detention ③

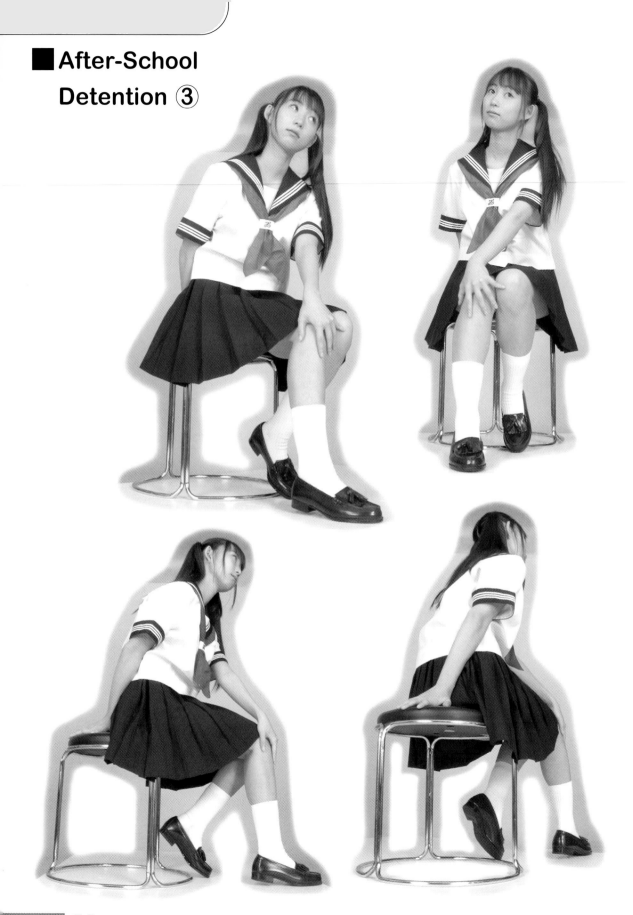

SCHOOL DAYS

Close-ups

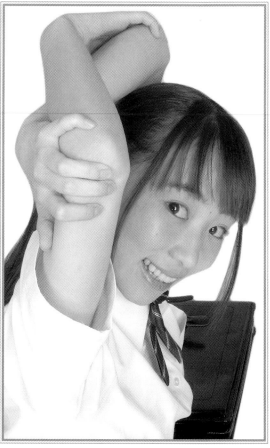

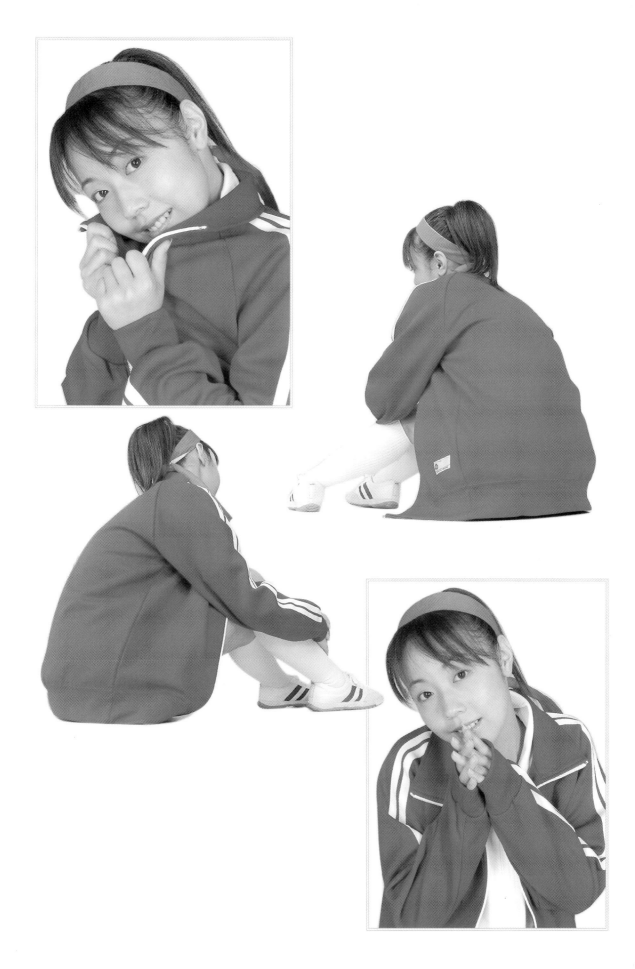

SECTION 3
PART-TIMER

Yuria Hidaka

Born: Dec. 15, 1982
Blood Type: AB
A girl with big dreams, Yuria has tested the waters of filmmaking, songwriting and modeling. Her full figure enhances her already commanding presence, and she displays a wide range of emotions as an actress.

Moe Sakurai

Born: July 25, 1978
Blood Type: AB
Moe's sweet smile matches her playful approach to life. Her cheerful personality and reputation as a hardworking professional has landed her several jobs as an MC at live events. She is also appearing on television more frequently, and aspires to be a newscaster.

When she's not attending classes or studying at home, the typical Japanese schoolgirl goes shopping for clothes and cosmetics, pours 100-yen coins into "print club" machines, treats herself to sugary crepes (so much for counting calories) and sings her heart out at the local karaoke club. All those activities cost money, though, which means she must also squeeze a part-time job into her busy schedule.

Two popular after-school jobs for young women in Japan are those of waitress at a quaint cafe and service maid at a European-style hotel. In this section we are introduced to Yuria Hidaka, who looks delectable in her form-fitting waitress uniform as she serves tasty pastries at a local cafe (pages 072-079). Upon entering the cafe and hearing Yuria's cheerful "*Irasshaimase!*" (Welcome!), you too will be drooling over the menu! Later, we'll get a sneak peek inside the hotel bedroom where perky part-timer Moe Sakurai (pages 080-087) is hard at work. (She's cleaning it, of course! What were you thinking?)

• •

Irasshaimase! 1-2

072-075

Serve With a Smile 1-2

076-079

• •

I Don't Do Windows! 1-2

080-083

Will That Be All? 1-2

084-087

• •

■Irasshaimase! ②

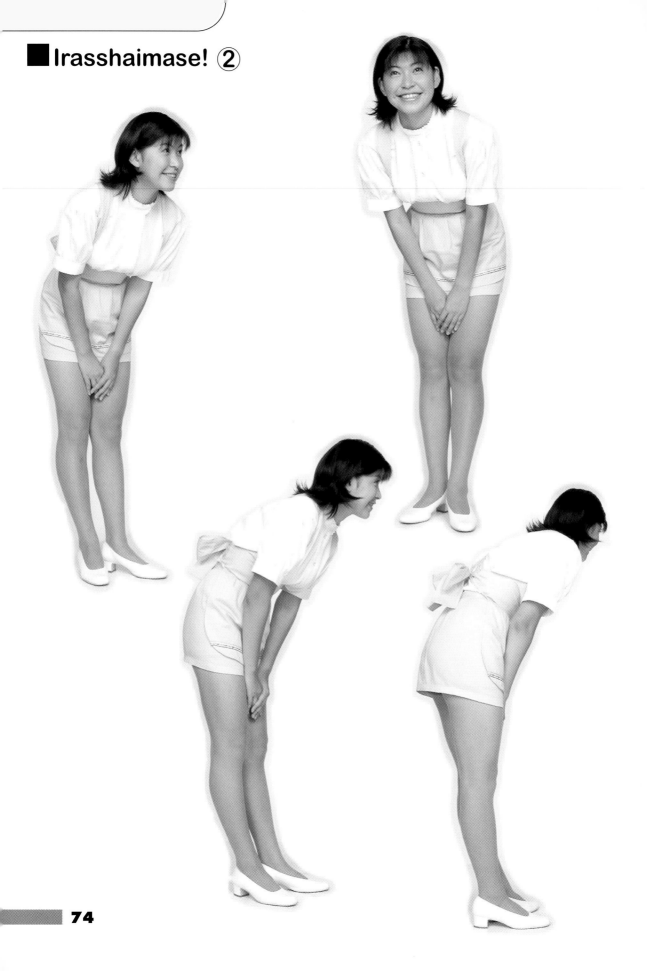

■Serve With a Smile ①

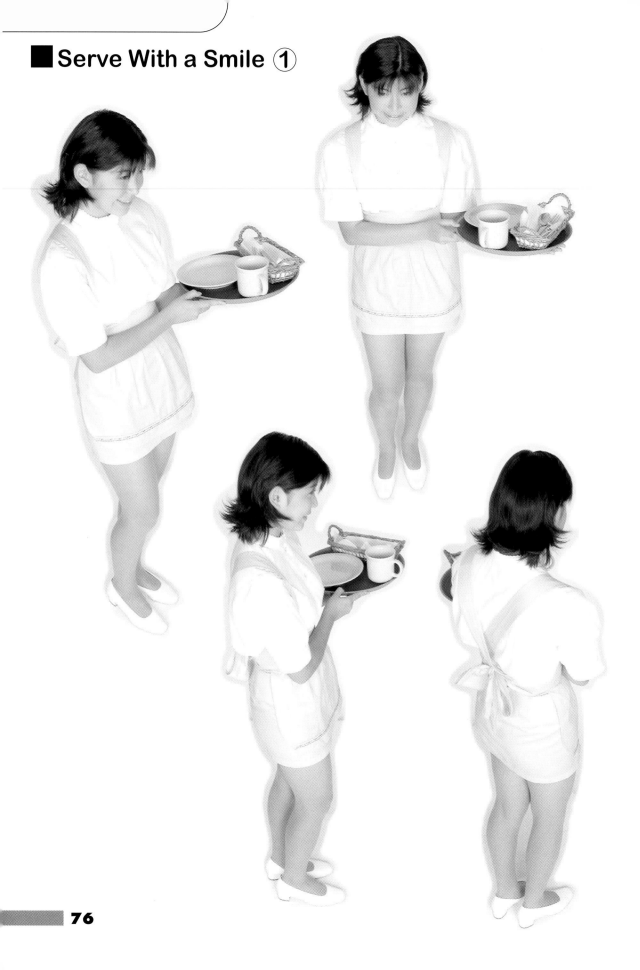

■I Don't Do Windows! ②

PART-TIMER
Close-ups

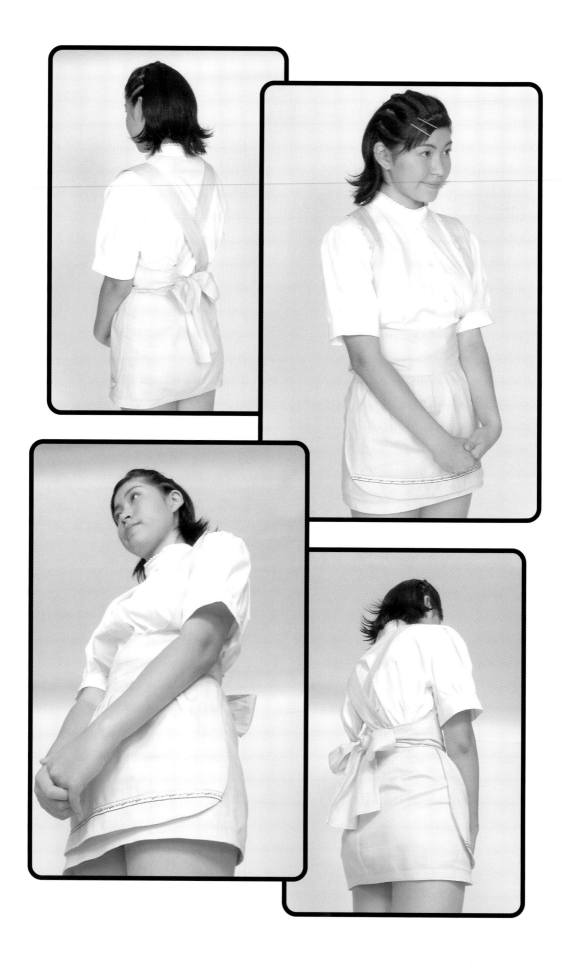

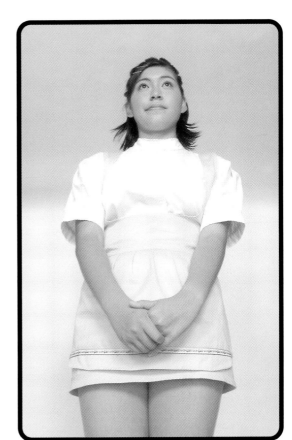

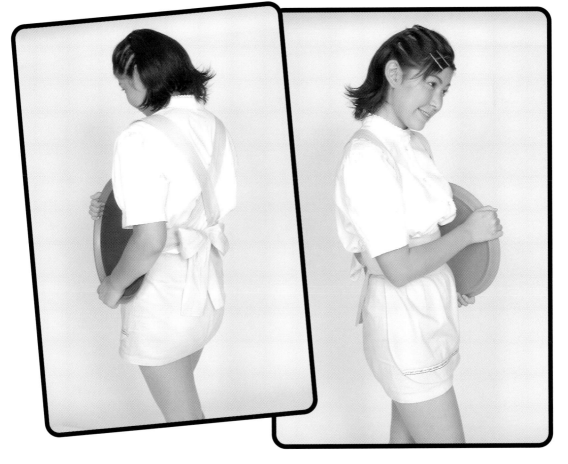

SECTION 4
TRADITIONAL GIRL

Riasu Arama

Born: Jan. 23, 1983
Blood Type: O
Gifted with a unique, friendly voice, Riasu enjoys popularity as the star of her own radio program. She also has appeared on television variety shows, and has lent her vocal talents to several videogame soundtracks. She occasionally poses for Japanese magazines.

Haruka Matsuki

Born: July 15, 1976
Blood Type: A
Always up for a challenge, Haruka has tackled projects in the areas of film, print and new media. As a model, she has appeared in several television commercials and elite magazines, and intends to build upon her already solid career.

An important part of every Japanese schoolgirl's education is learning how to be ladylike. And understanding the art of wearing a kimono (and its summertime cousin, the *yukata*) is a crucial first step. To paraphrase an old saying, "It isn't the girl who makes the kimono, it's the kimono that makes the *woman*." These classic garments epitomize the Japanese traditions of refined beauty and accentuated sexuality. It's no wonder that most young ladies can't wait for the chance to slip one on.

Here's our chance to meet Haruka Matsuki, whose traditional beauty is intensified by the way she carries herself during an after-school stroll through a tea garden (pages 102-105). Haruka also gives us a lesson in the proper way to sit *seiza*-style, with the legs tucked underneath and hands daintily clasped across the lap (pages 106-107). We'll also get reacquainted with Riasu Arama, whom we last met in after-school detention. Riasu looks adorable in her flower-print *yukata*(pages 108-113), even though the long summer day has left her rather *tsukareta* (wiped out).

Afternoon Stroll 1-2   Please Be Seated   Pleased to Meet You 1-2

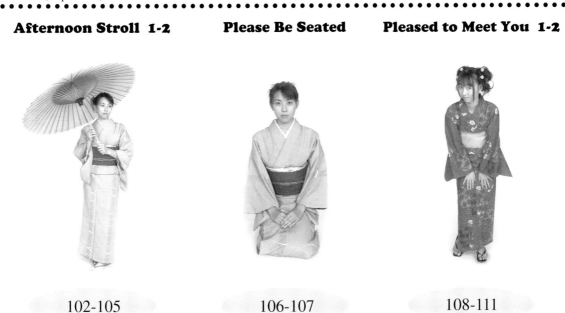

102-105   106-107   108-111

Tsukareta! 1   Tsukareta! 2   Elements of Style

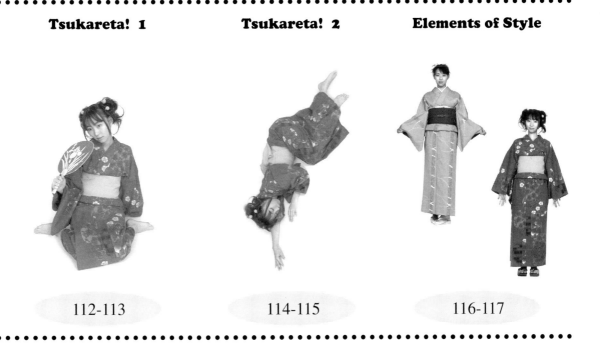

112-113   114-115   116-117

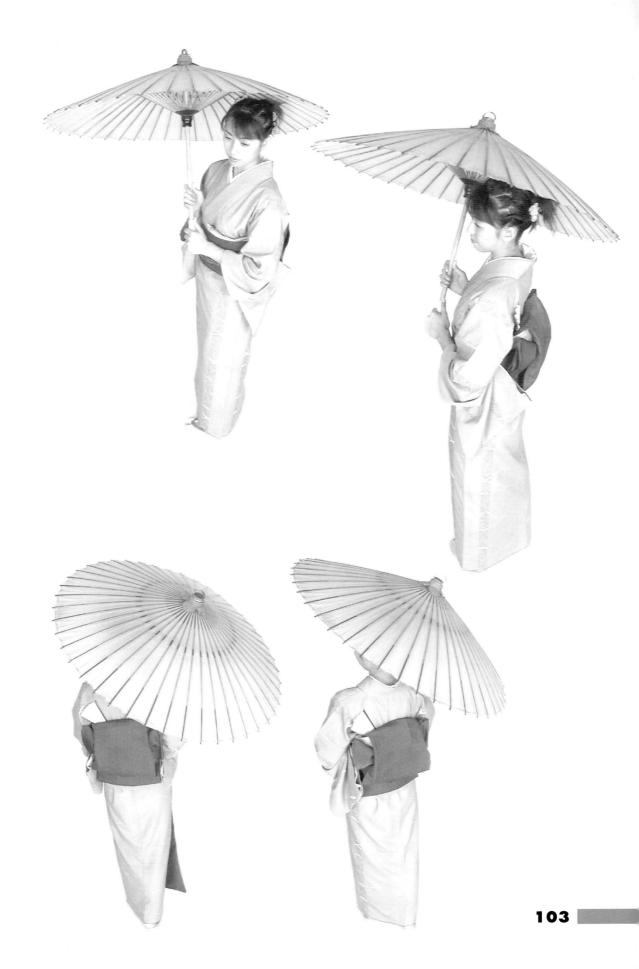

■Pleased to Meet You ①

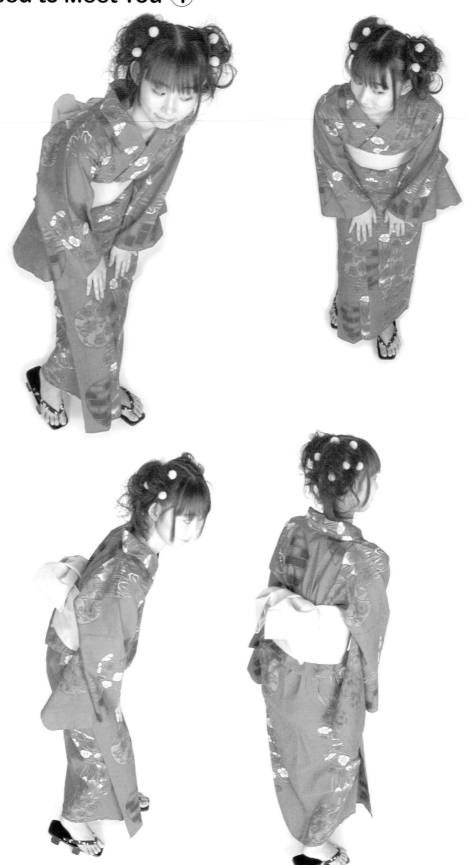

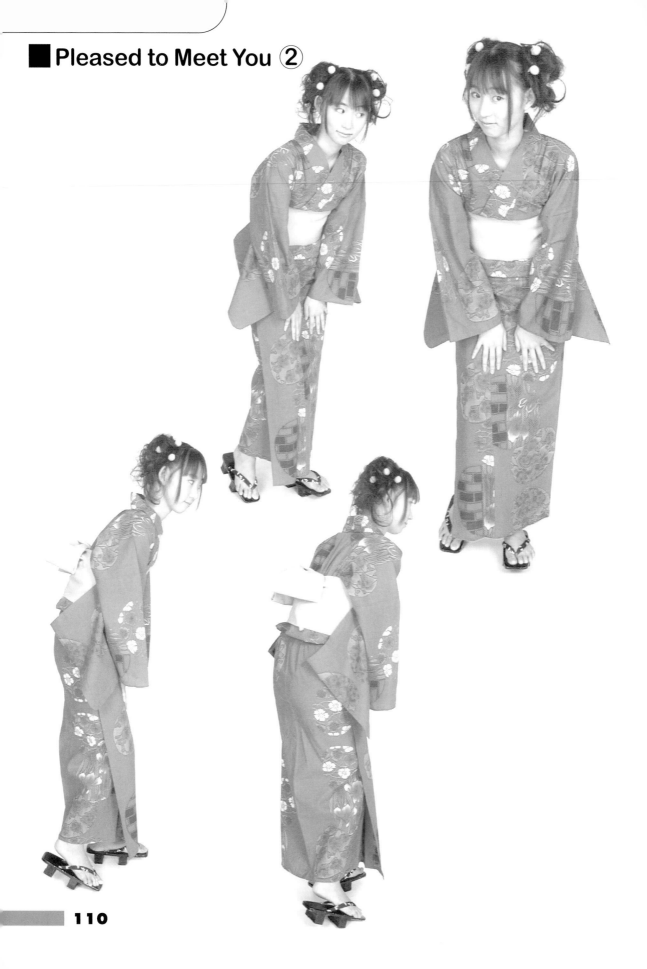

Elements of Style

More than a simple "robe," the formal kimono for women is an intricate dress consisting of an elegant exterior layer and several undergarments and accessories. Traditional kimono are made of silk and silk variations, while less-expensive variations feature cotton or synthetic fabrics. On the facing page are front and rear photographs of a *yukata* (summer kimono), with the Japanese names of the garment's elements written in both kanji and romanized letters, along with English translations. Subsequent pages in this section offer a closer look at kimono and *yukata*.

Today, the majority of Japanese wear Western-style clothing as they go about their daily routines. However, the kimono remains a popular choice for special occasions such as weddings, holidays and festivals. Kimono variations are also regularly worn by Shinto and Buddhist priests, shrine workers, sumo wrestlers, cultural performers and servers in upscale restaurants.

共衿（掛け衿）
Tomoeri (Kakeeri)
Over collar

帯
Obi
Sash

身八つ口
Miyatsukuchi
Opening under the sleeve

おはしょり
Ohasyori
Fold to support the obi

衣紋
Emon
Gap between the
collar and neck

上前
Uwamae
Outer skirt

背縫い
Senui
Back seam

つま先
Tsumasaki
Corner of hem

草履
Zori
Japanese sandals

袖
Sode
Sleeve

裾
Suso
Hem

TRADITIONAL GIRL
Close-ups

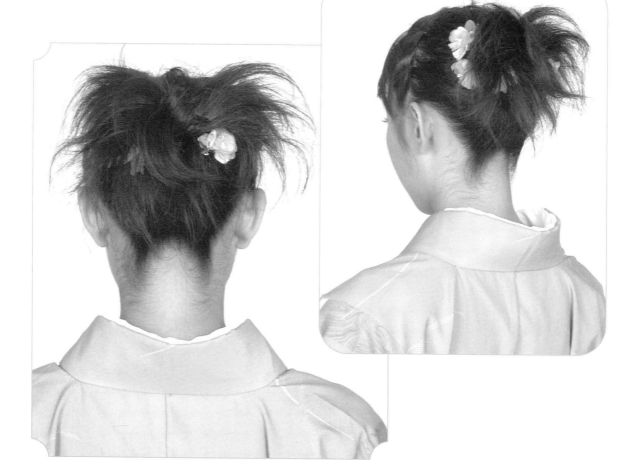

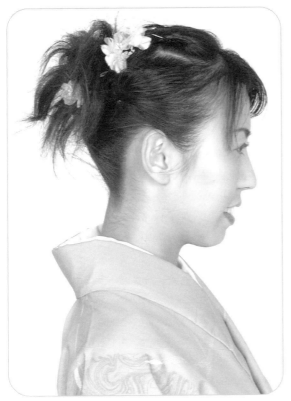

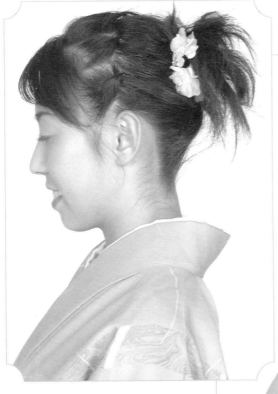

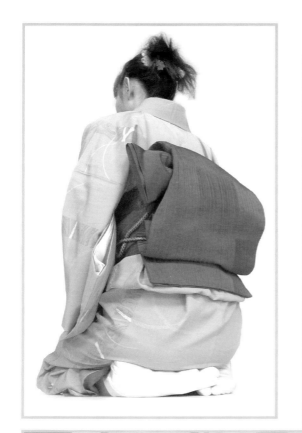

SECTION 5
NIGHTY-NIGHT

Mao Manabe

Born: May 21, 1985
Blood Type: O
When posing for this book, Nao actually dozed off during the sleeping scenes! Her innocent, easygoing personality is definitely contagious, and she has a large following to prove it. Her cute looks will serve her well as she pursues a career as a movie actress.

The homework is done, the midnight snack a distant memory. After a long, tedious day, it's time for our schoolgirl to unwind. Mom and Dad have been asleep for hours, and big brother (who also is studying for college entrance exams) can be heard snoring at his desk in the next room. Set the alarm clock for 6 a.m. and turn off the lights: We're gonna have a private pajama party!

Mao Manabe, who has been going strong since long before sunrise, shares her day with an overnight guest (pages 128-129), her beloved teddy bear named—what else?—Teddy! After that, a cup of soothing herbal tea and a few moments for intimate thoughts before falling fast asleep (pages 134-137). Sweet dreams!

Pajama Party

128-129

Tea Time

130-131

Private Moment

132-133

Sweet Dreams 1-2

134-137

■Pajama Party

■Tea Time

■Private Moment

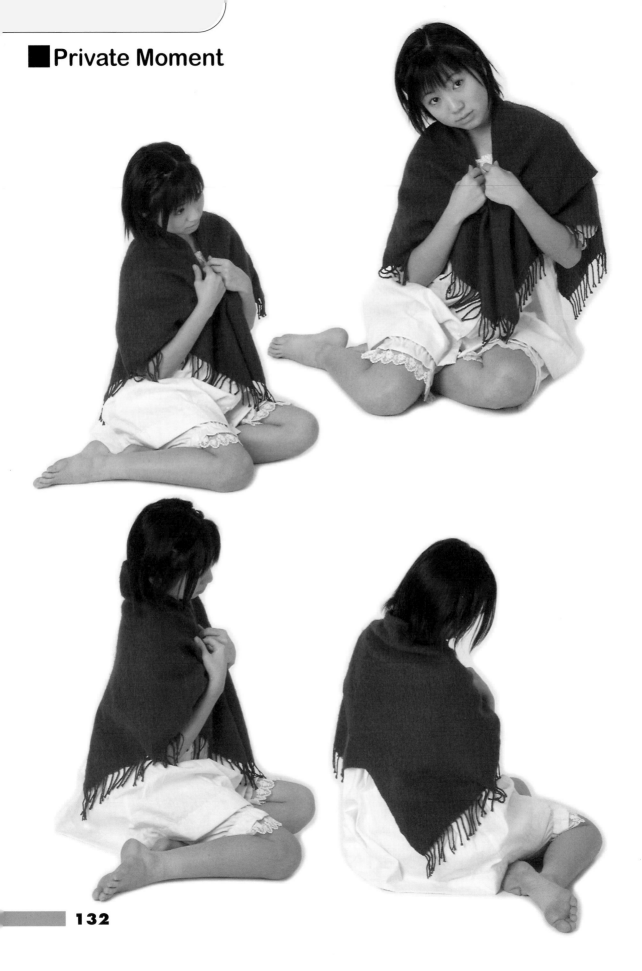

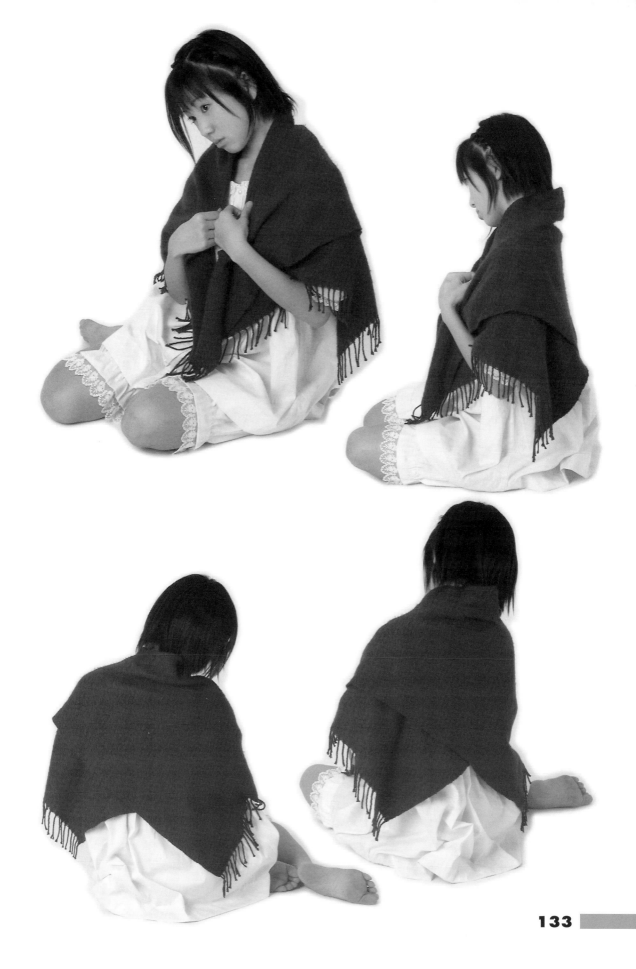

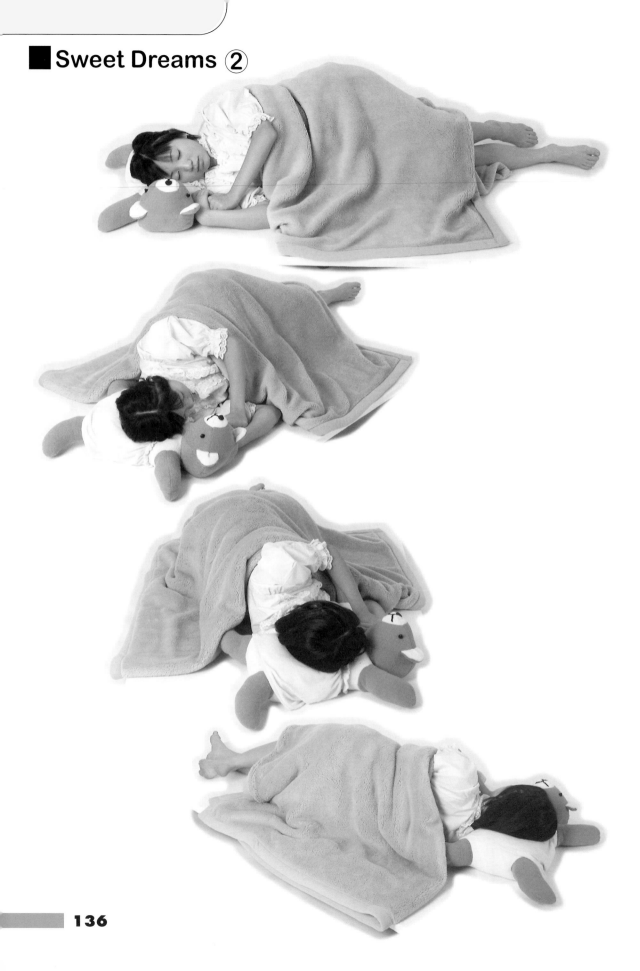

NIGHTY-NIGHT
Close-ups

www. MANGAUNIVERSITY .com

The place where your artistic education begins

To master the art of manga, you need the proper materials.
But you don't have to travel all the way to Japan to find them.
Visit us online at www.mangauniversity.com. It's where the pros go.